Stay!
Aunt

First Printing

ISBN 978-0-9984167-1-7

Book and Cover Design: Billy Mitchell, bybilly.com
Photography by Gabriel Coppola
Illustrations by Bobby Daye and Rosanna Iarusso

ONE MONKEY DON'T STOP NO SHOW...
UNLESS IT'S A ONE-MONKEY SHOW!

Weyman Thompson
Actor, Singer, Dancer, Director

Foreword

I've known Brenda Braxton since 1989. Seems like a long time ago, but at that point she had already established herself as a long-time working Broadway gypsy with many shows under her (dance) belt. (P.S. She still looks the same age now as when she first began! That's one secret none of us will learn from this book. It's called genes!) Anyhoo, we were doing Dreamgirls together in summer stock and she was playing Deena, one of the three leading roles. Now, she had already done Dreamgirls on Broadway, on national tour and internationally. This was just a three-week run at a theater in Connecticut. It had a much lower "fabulous factor" than all the productions she had done before, yet she treated it like she treats every other gig she has—with the highest level of respect.

The moment I want to tell you about happened on a Sunday. We were all living in not-so-great college dorms in Danbury, Connecticut, while we rehearsed six days a week. On Sunday afternoon we would all pile onto a train for the 90-minute ride back to our beloved New York City. We had one precious day off per week and the sooner we left Connecticut, the longer we could spend in our real homes. Rehearsal had ended that day and the cast went running to the station so they wouldn't miss the train and have to wait the additional hour.

I suddenly noticed the director going over to Brenda and telling her that he had a couple of things he wanted to talk about. Nothing of utmost importance, just show-related notes. I knew Brenda was dying to make that train because she was meeting her boyfriend in Manhattan that evening, and I was curious to see what she would do. I kept waiting for her to ask the director if they could continue the conversation during the next rehearsal or if she could call him that night and finish up. (She couldn't call him from the train because this was before cell phones!)

Well, instead of finding a way to leave so she could make that train, she simply stood there attentively. Not anxiously looking to the door, not nodding frantically so he'd finish. She just stood there, calmly taking in everything he was saying. Finally, he wrapped it up and told her he'd see her next week. As he walked away, she turned, grabbed her stuff and bolted for the train (which she made!). I remember thinking, "That woman is so professional. She didn't make the end of the day about herself and her not-unreasonable need to make the train back to the city. She knew the director wanted to speak to her, and she never let it be known that she was nervous she might miss her train. She knew that maybe what he had to say was fresh in his mind and he wouldn't have the same clarity if he waited to tell her."

I was so impressed that I remember it clearly to this day. I thought then that she could really teach actors how to work in the business. Well, now she finally is! This book is so perfect for anyone who wants to be in show business or stay in show business. No matter how many years you've been doing it, you should read it. Newcomers and old-timers can all learn from the gems on every page. As Brenda states from the beginning, there are so many more aspects to getting work and doing a good performance than just talent. There are many, many talented people in the business. But I know plenty (some of them Tony Award winners!) that don't get work because they never learned how to work well with others. This book tells you everything you need to know so you don't become unemployable.

Buy this book for yourself and for anyone you know who wants a successful show business career. It tells it like it is with humor, honesty, warmth and truth. The sooner you learn these skills, the longer your career will last. And take it from Brenda. After all, she's been working steadily since 1865 (sorry, Brenda, I had to!).

Seth Rudetsky
Actor, Musician, Author
Host, SiriusXM Radio

Acknowledgments

When I decided to write this book, once again I was reminded of how blessed I am with friends and family who have always been there for me. This book now gives me the opportunity to thank and honor everyone who has stood by me for all these 60 years of my life and 40 years of professional life. When I announced my idea for this book, everyone agreed it was well overdue!

Thank you to my mother, Lillian Braxton, who has been my biggest fan. She showed me from a young age how to believe I could do just about any and everything. Her words "We are descendants of kings and queens" forever rings in my ears and informs everything I do. Thanks to my aunt and cousin, Naomi Shelnut and Stacey Shelnut-Hendrick, for the love and support.

I thank everyone who has lent their time to this book. To Bobby Daye and Rosana Iarusso, thank you for the wonderful illustrations. Thank you, Billy Mitchell, for taking the wheel, putting this book in solid form and showing me the self-publishing ropes! Thanks to Amy Scott for your editing expertise and to Gabriel Coppolla—my cover photo is everything! To all my wonderful friends, old and new, who lent their quotes and

experiences to make The Little Black Book of Backstage Etiquette
a success: Bebe Neuwirth, Zane Mark, e'Marcus Harper-Short,
David Hyslop, Gregory Butler, Jermaine Brown Jr., Lee Summers,
Scott Mortimer, Sarah Greenstone, Jackie Sayles, Ogre, Rachel
Blavatnik, Destinee Rea and Kenneth Hanson. Last but not least,
thank you Seth Rudetsky for the wonderful foreword, but most
importantly for your friendship and respect! Keep those crunch-
es going! (waaaaaah)

And now for my community, whom I love and respect and
just want to thank in general. Because every single time I come
up with an idea for something you're always there to say, "How
can I help?!"

Thank you to: Terry Burrell, Allison Williams-Foster, Brenda
Pressley, Chita Rivera, Babs Winn, Mary Mossburg, LaChanz,
Rita Wilson, Adrian Bailey, Shaun Derrick, Rhonda Ridley,
Bernard Dotson, Bianca Marroquin, Marquitta Graham, Geneva
Vivino, James Seol, Dustin Cross, Frederick B. Owens, Kenneth
Roberson, Sabra Richardson, Deb Walton-Hill, Dan LoBuono,
Marva Hicks-Taha, Adriane Lenox, Jeremy Daniel, Robert Tatad,
Rick Martinez, Robin C. Green, Felicia Polk, Sonia Alleyne, Gail
Young, Shawn Emamjomeh, Michele Sanford, Lindsey Roginski,
Ellis Porter, DeLee Lively, Natasha Boyd, Elizabeth Dane, Joe
Wilson Jr., Lillias White, Andrew Kato, Randy Slovacek, Eugene
R. Palmore, Leslie Stifelman, Melissa Rae Mahon and Donna
Marie Asbury.

STAY FIERCE!

The Little Black Book of Backstage Etiquette

BY
Brenda Braxton

Introduction

Finally: a book that just might be the secret to having a long-lasting theater career! You see, The Little Black Book of Backstage Etiquette is the weapon you need to thrive and survive in this crazy arena called Show Business. Because sometimes it might not be solely about your talent; sometimes it's about your reputation. How easy you are to work with. Or even whether you're known for good work ethics.

Now I know some of you talented thespians might be saying, "Backstage etiquette...yeah right. I'll have you know I just graduated from (feel free to insert your alma mater) with a degree in theater!" Believe it or not, sometimes that's not enough. Don't get me wrong. School is an amazing tool to help navigate this business. I applaud anyone who has the courage, tenacity and strength to take the time for that journey in learning the craft of acting, dancing and performing. The thing is, there's one part of the journey that (to my knowledge) is not being taught, and there are some things you really won't learn until you are actually in the theater.

While writing this book I've had a fabulous run in The Wiz at the Maltz Jupiter Theatre in Jupiter, Florida, a production of

After Midnight on Norwegian Cruise Line and participated in Playbill's Broadway on the High Seas 7, performing with Seth Rudetsky, Chita Rivera, Faith Prince, Adam Pascal and a host of other Broadway veterans. During this time I worked with several young performers and was pleasantly surprised at their professionalism and dedication. The Little Black Book of Backstage Etiquette was born out of a few of those fresh young actors asking me a simple question: How have you been able to stay relevant in show business (theater in particular) for over 40 years?

I was stunned to find that they felt their generation was one that feels "entitled" to everything and that this bothered them. They shared with me that young performers nowadays feel they have arrived once they book their first show, and they were curious about how they could break away from that notion and really have a full and positive theater experience that would keep taking them to the next level. I applaud them for asking questions and wanting to do better. Their curiosity was so refreshing it led me to share some of my backstage stories and experiences, such as how I literally started out in the chorus and worked my way up to leading lady and Tony Award nominee. Or how launching my own production company allowed me to see theater from the other side, as a producer. Not to mention coming up in a time when for some jobs I had to actually supply my own makeup, hair care products and hosiery because none was provided for brown-skinned dancers.

Those situations could have made me very bitter and difficult to work with. Instead, they made me seek out other ways of showing my talents and surviving, such as learning how to run a spotlight or being a production assistant on a Broadway show. Knowing how to treat others in those situations was priceless because it gave me a close-up look at life not just from the side of the performer, but from all aspects of theater and what it takes to make a show successful.

Yes, theater is about talent, but it's also about what kind of person you are and how you treat your fellow performers and coworkers whose work and contributions help make theater a wonderful and enchanting place to live and work.

This book is an insight into what to expect and how to handle some of the common-sense situations that might arise once you finally book a show. This book can also transcend into everyday workplace situations as well. It's a book that I hope will be handed down by stage managers on the first day of rehearsals and by teachers; read in performing arts schools, acting classes and dance classes; given as a gift to that artist you support; and read by anyone looking forward to a career in theater. The Little Black Book of Backstage Etiquette is the icing on the cake of a successful career in theater.

Welcome to EMERALD CITY!

So you've just booked your first show?

You've been through and survived the audition process (and possible callbacks) and come out on the other side. That queasy feeling in the pit of your stomach has subsided and all is right with the world once again. Well. Now the work, fun and challenges really begin.

Not only do you have to learn your lines, choreography, lyrics and blocking, you also have to learn what I like to call Backstage Etiquette or "How To Live and Work Backstage with Others (Often in Tight Spaces) without Killing Anyone." This book teaches you a few things you need to know about backstage etiquette and the house rules of the theater. It gives you a first-hand idea of some things that might not have been covered in your classes at school or even in your life up to this point, including experiences and issues that often come up only once you're in the actual backstage theater world. While this book attempts to explain as we go along many terms you might not have heard before, at the back of the book there is a Glossary of Theater Terms and an Etiquette at a Glance list that you might find helpful.

The added beauty of this book is that since many artists

might work temp jobs between theater gigs, the information I'm sharing here can be used for any work venue and/or life in general. At the end of the day, The Little Black Book of Backstage Etiquette is all about respect, and respect is important in any job or career.

If you were lucky enough to go to a performing arts school, you may feel you have an "advantage" over those who did not. But I think until you've actually been out here in the trenches, you really have no idea what it takes.

Don't get me wrong—education is important. Knowing how to break down a scene, pull from emotions or find the character's arch is extremely valuable, but there are a host of other issues that occur even before you hit the stage or that first paying audience arrives.

Now, who am I, you ask? WOW! Where do I begin?

Here's a brief herstory of Brenda Braxton, singer, dancer, actor, producer, entrepreneur and now author! It's hard to believe, but 2016 marks my 40th year in professional theater! I know—I look good, right? Anyhoo, I call myself a real gypsy showgirl because there aren't many of us left who can honestly say they worked their way up from a chorus girl to leading lady! It has been a long journey, but I'm still here, and it's not over yet!

I grew up in the Bronx and went to the High School of Performing Arts (the old FAME building, as they call it). I have had the pleasure of performing on Broadway as Velma Kelly in CHICAGO The Musical, sharing the stage with Usher, Rita

Wilson, Bebe Neuwirth, Lisa Rinna and Brian McKnight.

I was nominated for a Tony Award in 1995 for my starring role on Broadway in Smokey Joe's Cafe and received the NAACP Theater Award, Chicago's Jefferson Award and a Grammy for Best Musical Show Album. A few of my other Broadway credits are Cats, Legs Diamond with Peter Allen (you might want to Google him), the original Dreamgirls and Jelly's Last Jam alongside Gregory Hines and Savion Glover.

I attended the City College of New York (CCNY) the year they opened the Leonard Davis Center for the Performing Arts, but once I got a taste of Broadway just a year later, that was it! I left school for the Great White Way and the rest is history. My first Broadway show was the African-American version of Guys and Dolls starring Robert Guillaume, Ken Page and many other talented up-and-comers. That was in 1976. I had no idea what to do or how to act, but I watched and learned. I was so green that I had auditioned for the job of swing dancer without even knowing what a swing dancer did!

Back then, in order to learn what shows were auditioning, you would have to skim through two weekly papers, Backstage and Showbiz. These publications would advertise all the new shows, classes you could take, photographers offering special prices for head shots and upcoming auditions. I went to what is known as an open call (an audition that anyone can attend) and there were over 200 dancers.

At that time, you actually auditioned on a Broadway stage

with all the other dancers and singers watching, and the entire production team (director, choreographer, stage manager) seated in the audience.

Nowadays, most auditions are done in studios or even by video! I'll never forget that I sang "What the World Needs Now" because that's what I had chosen in my high school musical theater class with Ms. Malinka! Well, needless to say it paid off: I was hired as the only female "swing"!

It was a whole new world. School was great, but until I actually booked my first show and stepped into rehearsal, I had no idea what I was in for. But I was like a sponge. Ready for anything and not afraid to ask questions.

For those of you who don't know what a swing dancer is, it's an understudy for the chorus members, mostly the dancers. Most of the time, a male swing is hired to cover the men and a female swing for the women. A few years later, in the original production of Dreamgirls on Broadway, I found myself in a swing position where I covered both men and women in the company. Now that was a challenge!

When Guys and Dolls closed I was blessed to join a theater company at the Urban Arts Corps. There's nothing like working for little to no money but loving what you do. I worked with Vinnette Carroll, the first African-American woman to direct a Broadway play. I have fond memories of my time there, including the times we only had enough money to travel one way for rehearsal so we walked 60 blocks home, then we pooled our unemployment money so everyone could eat.

I shared a small one-bedroom apartment on the Upper West Side with two roommates, three dogs and one snake. (You'll have to read my memoir for more on that. But I digress!) During that time I also performed in the movie The Wiz, starring Diana Ross and Michael Jackson. I'll never forget seeing Michael Jackson the first time he danced "Ease on Down the Road" with Diana Ross... Priceless. And filming the scene when there were 400 of us dancers, singers and models in the freezing cold down at the old World Trade Center. When I look back on those years and experiences, I realize I was paying my dues. I wouldn't give up those days for anything!

Everything I learned in my time at the Urban Arts Corps and on Broadway in my first show helped me survive working with other performers, in small spaces and in general. Each show has taught me lessons I feel should be passed down to the next generation of performers. This book is about one lesson that I don't think has been taught in any performing arts school or theater workshop, and that is backstage etiquette.

It's all about the importance of knowing and respecting the jobs of everyone involved in this production you are blessed to be a part of, from the person at the stage door (do you even know his/her name?) to the actors you share your dressing room with, to the people who run the spotlights, the person who cleans your dressing room, your dresser who helps you with your costume and even the ushers who seat the audience members. Backstage etiquette is a dying knowledge and way of life that will get lost in all the "entitlement" noise unless it's handed down to new generations.

One of the talented 24-year-old up-and-coming performers I worked with shared his take on why this book is important:

> *I spend a lot of time talking with Brenda about how different our generations are, in regards to the support that we receive(d) and the behavior we witness from our peers. It is key for us artists to remember: No matter how broad the résumé or how long you've been in the business, etiquette and respect for one another is essential. In the end, we're in this small community together and we should make our time worthwhile. A negative trait that's stirring within my generation that is rather palpable is the sense of entitlement. It blows my mind to see how one can carry themselves, or treat others just because they've booked a few shows. Manners are thrown out the window and etiquette is no longer key. In any case, if I ever feel entitlement sneaking up behind me, I blatantly ask myself, who do you think you are, and what have you done to act so privileged? It seems "I must be THE star" is seeping into our aura, minds and egos and veils the primary purpose of art. Art is so much more; art is present; it is life; it is existence; it is inspiration; it is breath. Art simply IS.*
>
> *I believe this book is very insightful and refreshing for newcomers to the theater community AND the "veterans." Thank you, Brenda, for this book and allowing me to lend my voice to our community.*

Jermaine Brown Jr.
After Midnight
Norwegian Cruise Line

Throughout this book you'll find comments by people actually working in the various departments that you'll have contact with. There were two main questions I asked the wonderful people who lent their experiences and suggestions: 1) In your department, what are your pet peeves with performers? 2) What advice would you give new performers to improve relations in the theater?

I hope their experience and stories give you a little insight to the importance of respect and being a team player behind the scenes in any venue. The Little Black Book of Backstage Etiquette shares thoughts, experiences and suggestions from those of us who have been there, done that. Some of the advice might seem like common sense, but as they say, "Sometimes common sense ain't all that common."

As the following comments show, backstage etiquette begins the moment you sit down for the first table read. A table read is usually on the first day of rehearsal. Once the meet and greet is over, the cast and creative team will sit around the table and just read through the script to finally give a general sense of what the show sounds like before "putting it on its feet" (starting rehearsals).

The situation described by this performer is why I'm a firm

believer that all table reads should be done with old-fashioned paper scripts and pencils. This way everyone is on the same page and making whatever notes/changes are needed.

Everyone was excited for the first table read before getting on our feet. This was an iconic show and we were proud to have been cast in the Broadway revival. This was not my first Broadway show but I'm always happy to see/ meet the talented people I'll be performing with and the magic we can make together. Unfortunately, I was horrified to see that as we were reading through the script many of the ensemble performers were on their phones texting, tweeting and checking messages. This is so disrespectful on so many levels. Not only is it distracting to others, but it means you're not fully present to what's going on. You do yourself such a disservice in the process of forming your show. I realized these performers were only interested in what they had to do in the show and not the importance of the show in its entirety. My advice to new/young performers is to be present and learn your craft at every moment in the process. It's not enough to just be physically present. You have to have your head in the game from day one!

Turn your phone off and leave it in your bag until your break. If you're a serious performer (even starting out in the ensemble), you should know that what you bring to the table is equally as important or you would not have been hired.

The world won't stop turning because you didn't answer that tweet, text or Facebook post, but you might not be hired for that next show if the powers that be see you're disinterested and have a poor work ethic. Theater is a very small community and nine times out of ten you will work with some of these people again.

Anonymous Performer

My 40+ years in this business have not only allowed me to experience this wonderful business from different angles and perspectives, but I've met amazing friends and fellow cast mates who have done the same. We have watched one another grow from chorus members to Broadway directors, producers, choreographers, Tony Award winners, teachers and more. We learned this business is not about being a one-hit wonder. It's about longevity and staying relevant. It's not about arriving at stardom as quickly as possible, but the journey and what you can learn along the way. It's about building bridges and lasting friends and coworkers. I am proud to say I still have friends and cast mates I met in my first Broadway show back in 1976! We are constantly calling one another and encouraging each other because we know what it took for us to get where we are.

Having performed on Broadway in the '80s and maintained a consistent career in New York theater, producing, directing, acting in film and TV since that time—and presently having been awarded a scholarship to earn an MFA in writing for Musical Theatre from NYU/Tisch School of the Arts after the age of 50—it is evident my career spans from the professional to the academic and from the old school to the new school. Before I expound on any pet peeves, I would like to acknowledge that there are many amazing young people whose parents, teachers and/or personal journeys have guided them into being terrific human beings and gifted artists who brightly beam as the future of our industry. I am also most encouraged when I observe how more and more young people, particularly those of color, have a healthy sense of entitlement to social justice and equality—more, perhaps, than any previous generation.

The most important thing that young people must realize is that this business is tiny and the way people most often put projects together is by asking those whom they know and trust to participate.

No matter how high you sing, how many pirouettes you do or if you can out-Streep Meryl, if your reputation is bad (a.k.a. stank), forget about it.

Not only is it a privilege to perform for the public, but it is also a privilege to create with the brilliant people who make it happen. Any creative team faced with bringing a new script to life is faced with a daunting challenge; the last thing they need is a performer with a bad attitude who is late, absent, resistant or blocking the creative process because they feel it's all about them, their moment or how they will shine. I have learned to sniff those people out ASAP and to quickly let them know they are optional in the process. No matter who they are I will just make the replacement. I am not a therapist; I am an artist. I have repeatedly learned that the creation of art is through discovery. Our job is to remain flexible within the varied disciplines and at all costs to remain gracious, even when we do not agree. Our next 10 jobs or our entire careers *could depend upon it.*

I would argue that many (not all, thank the stars) young people—having been raised watching television and with their heads buried in smartphones, video games and iPads—have been "Kardashianized" and have thus lost the concept of effort equaling achievement.

They also have not been socialized in the manner people were socialized prior to the Internet. "Socialized" meaning knowing the importance of an action as simple as saying "hello" or "goodbye" to coworkers, cast mates or classmates as they enter or exit a room. This simple act of humanity appears to be an endangered social expectation. Also the basic understanding that the "stank face" and eye rolling shown after receiving a critique from a teacher, director, choreographer or anyone in a position of authority is not an anonymous comment hidden behind a laptop screen. I can see you, Blanche, and now I have to use my energy to ignore or excuse you.

In many young people there is a basic lack of understanding of their own facial expressions and body language, and a general unawareness of what signals they are sending out and what signals they are missing. Some young inexperienced people feel that being nasty, curt and/or condescending will demonstrate wisdom and confidence. Sadly, it will only demonstrate why it will be the last time I will work with them.

That said, my biggest pet peeve with the younger generation is their unhealthy sense of entitlement. Millennials often feel they are entitled to fly before they even have wings. As a baby-booming professional in a millennial world, I recall how this change in perspective was slowly revealed to me. It crept into my awareness like the sudden arrival of crackheads in the 1990s, a new, unattractive breed of dysfunctional beings caused by a new societal addiction: the Internet. I remember my first time witnessing an unprecedented lack of reality, which in hindsight was symptomatic of repeated exposure to music videos, reality TV, the Internet and social media.

These new cyber "drugs" were infecting a generation of dreamers. In 2007 (when Rihanna's "Umbrella" was climbing the charts), I asked a young man what he would like to do with his life. He answered, "I want to become famous from dancing; it worked for Jennifer Lopez, it can work for me." He had never even taken a single dance class. Classes on the craft of acting, singing and dancing in my day had been replaced with YouTube views and Facebook likes.

In conclusion, here are a few final thoughts on practices and protocols:

- *Please don't rely on a tablet and social media for your sole source of communication; please use a phone.*

- *In rehearsals, don't think you can be blocked by a director by having your script on an iPad in a PDF document. You can't write down your notes quickly, and who has time for you to recharge your device if needed?*

- *Another major pet peeve as a director is having to ask young people to write down their blocking or their notes on their performance, then not seeing the note executed. Back in my day, if you came in and did not show you had taken and remembered the note you were given, you could be fired!*

- *No texting in rehearsals. Duh?*

- *I can't believe I have to type this next one, but just in case someone needs to be told, please do not take a phone call and have a full-out conversation within earshot of rehearsing cast mates.*

- *If you have ADD or some other modern condition that hinders your ability to be silent or still, tell your director or stage manager early in the process so he or she can be supportive.*

- *Do not get up and walk out of the rehearsal room without telling the stage manager where you are going—and if it is between your union breaks, do so only if it is an emergency.*

- *If you are union and find yourself working with non-union people, try to bring them up to your level of professional expectation and discipline; do not allow them to bring you down to theirs.*

As Whoopi Goldberg said on The View, "There is no old school, new school, there is professional and unprofessional." If you are ever unsure about any practices and protocols, never be afraid to ask; that is how we all learn.

Now, have a happy career in the best business in the world!

Lee Summers
Actor, Director
MFA, NYU School of the Arts

In this time of iPads and all sorts of bells and whistles, I know young performers feel it's not a big deal how they write their notes and blocking. All I can say is just try it. There's something about the feel of having your paper script and pencil in hand and writing down direction that really puts you in the moment of the entire experience. It allows you to focus, and many directors appreciate when you are with them mentally, physically and sometimes emotionally (depending on the piece). Having to wait for you to go back, press delete, re-type, etc. can often ruin the flow of the creative process and working in the moment.

It can be off-putting to a director to have to roll back their energy when performers aren't engaged and haven't been following them closely. Yes, it's true, a lot of directors appreciate it when artists make the attempt to get inside their heads and grasp their vision, and good artists do this well. If you are lucky enough to get into a piece that is being workshopped, it is doubly important that you are keeping up with the creative energy and flow of the director, music arranger and choreographer. You don't want to be guilty of hindering the creative flow of someone on the creative team by not being fully engaged—trust me, you don't. Take your work seriously and arrange your life so that, at least for the time that you are in the room, nothing else exists except what you are being directed/asked to do. Pay full attention the entire time and be ready to execute on a dime; it may even earn you a nice little feature moment.

e'Marcus Harper-Short
Musical Director
Black Nativity

Stage Door Person

I often say the stage door person is like the bouncer at Studio 54 back in the '70s: you have to get past them in order to get in. I can hear you now, "Stage doorman? He sits at the door, takes messages and signs for packages. What's the big deal?" Well, here's the big deal.

In 1995, while I was performing on Broadway in Smokey Joe's Cafe, I attracted a fan who was a bit more than I could handle. He was in prison and went from sending me letters to actually showing up at the theater upon his release! Needless to say, it was

not a good or safe situation.

Our doorman at the time, Neil Perez, was ever vigilant to the situation and was able to handle it in a way that diffused any trouble that might have ensued. Now you might think that was his job, but not necessarily. You see, I feel if I hadn't forged a relationship of respect and acknowledgment of his contribution to the show, he could have very well taken the attitude that handling this fan was not part of his job description.

Another reason to get to know your door person is that he or she might have amazing stories to share from a long history as one of the "gate keepers" of Broadway. That was the case when I did Dreamgirls at the Imperial Theater. The late Joe Battle was known for his love of the theater and the performers who passed through his stage door. There's also Rosie at the Shubert—now she has stories!

Even if you don't/can't remember their names (and I have to admit I sometimes have that problem), make sure you at least acknowledge them. Say please and thank you. Trust me, it matters, and a little respect goes a long way.

Every day we work with people who have a wide range of experience under their belt. The Broadway theater stage door person is much like that person you might run across at your job who has been there for many years. Sometimes it pays to acknowledge their presence and the time they have been at their job. Don't just assume they have nothing to offer or common courtesy is not warranted.

Stage Manager

I laugh and cringe as I write this section because I haven't always been the best to stage management. But, I lived and learned, so that today I can write about the importance of respecting management. These people are often on the production from day one, many times even before you are cast in the show. They know the show from top to bottom. If they don't know the answers to your questions, they'll find out in a hurry (at least the good ones will). Most Broadway shows have three stage managers: a Production Stage Manager (PSM) and two assistants (ASM).

You might even have a production assistant, which was

HALF HOUR!
AT TONIGHT'S
PERFORMANCE, THE
ROLE OF ...

a title I held on the Broadway production of Lena Horne: The Lady and Her Music (yes, I've pretty much done it all). I learned early in my career to say yes to everything that had to do with learning the ins and outs of theater. So production assistant it was! I was in charge of all the little things, from getting coffee to helping with the seating chart for the opening-night party to retyping Ms. Horne's lyrics to make them easier to read in rehearsals. There were no computers to cut and paste back then, so it was all done with a typewriter. I remember being up until the wee hours of the morning typing lyrics and having to use carbon paper! (Some of you might have to look that up!)

Some Off-Broadway shows have fewer stage managers, sometimes just a PSM and an assistant who doubles as a stagehand— yes, that happens too!

No matter the number of stage managers on your production, you should show the same respect and patience to all. Their jobs can become quite stressful at times, especially when you start to tech the show. Stage managers often survive on nothing but coffee and oxygen for days at a time on 10 out of 12 days. Once you've moved from your rehearsal space into the theater and the process of lighting scenes and dance numbers begins, a performer is allowed to be called to work 10 hours out of a 12-hour rehearsal day. But for most stage managers, it can turn into an around-the-clock situation! If you pay attention, you'll notice that they will be at the theater when you arrive and still be there when you leave for the night.

Respect them because oftentimes they've been doing what they do a lot longer than you have even been in show business. So close your mouth, listen and learn. If you're onstage being lit, stay where you're placed. Sometimes lighting a show is a long process and you're standing for hours (with your Equity breaks, of course), so be prepared for it. Be where you're supposed to be. When asked to move, move with a purpose. If you're called in for the day and you never get to your scene, oh well. You are being paid to be there and this is the business you chose to be in, so enjoy the journey. No one really wants to hear you bitch and moan!

The mindset of new actors must start with the basics. Be on time—actually, be early! Don't be known for getting to work just in time. Come to work and do your eight shows a week. You have to be known as a person that comes to work. Once you're known as a person that won't/ can't do eight shows a week, you've killed your career. Give the same performance for every show. People should never be able to say, "You should come on Saturday; he/she's better at the end of the week."

Also know that actors don't give notes to other actors. Go to your stage manager or dance captain if you have feedback. Know your place. If your name isn't selling tickets, you won't have much say in anything.

One other thing I hate is an actor that's not gracious to audience members at the stage door after the show. Greeting the audience comes with the territory. I can understand sometimes not being able to stand and sign EVERYONE'S Playbill, but you should be gracious.

In a nutshell, I feel if you don't master the basics, your entire career can be in jeopardy, especially as an African-American performer. There aren't as many shows to choose from so it's crucial to be known as a team player.

Kenneth Hanson
Production Stage Manager
Smokey Joe's Cafe, The Wiz, Bubbling Brown Sugar

Mr. Hanson also shared with me that one problem is actors signing in before the half-hour call (the time everyone is required to sign in at the theater and begin preparing for the show) and then saying they're just going to "run out to the store." That is a big no-no. Not only is it illegal, but it also puts the show in jeopardy if—God forbid—something happens to you on the street and you're unable to return. That goes for when you're on the road as well: on your day off, you cannot leave the city you're in without informing your stage manager. Simply put, leaving town without telling anyone puts the production in danger if there is no one to cover you in your absence.

I also agree with him that ladies (especially the star of the show) should not exit the theater looking like a bag lady! I know some might say, "Well, I just left my blood, sweat and tears on the stage. What more do they want?" But that's such a lazy thought! It doesn't take anything to make yourself presentable. Don't just smear off your make-up and throw a hat on. If you don't have time to remove lashes and make-up properly, invest in a nice pair of sunglasses and a colorful scarf. Trust me: it makes a big difference to the people who have paid to see you.

Another stage manager I talked with emphasized the need to keep your stage manager informed of your availability.

As an actor who has been both an understudy and a swing dancer, I know firsthand how it feels when you find out at the last minute that you're on! Unless an emergency happens during the show, ample notice should be given to stage management.

It's becoming more and more common practice for actors to "text out" sick or injured rather than call out.

If you're sick, I really appreciate a phone call—not only so I can understand the severity of the situation, but also if we're in a possible bind with a number of people out, you're at least aware of the situation and can decide whether, given the circumstances, you could actually make it through a show without further injuring yourself.

I don't need to know early in the morning that you "might" be out on a given day. If you're going to call, do it to call out sick rather than give me a status update on your health. In most cases, I'm not going to contact your understudy unless I'm certain you are out. That said, if we are early in previews or have a new understudy and are perhaps more vulnerable than usual, I do appreciate a heads up.

I always appreciate a focused understudy rehearsal. There's nothing more annoying than gathering together for an understudy rehearsal where actors are fooling around or goofing off. It doesn't support the newer understudies and is a waste of everybody's time. Also along these lines, always stay focused at put-in rehearsals. The new cast member deserves your full attention and energy; this is a time to give your full support to them rather than a time to socialize off in the corner with the other cast members.

When in rehearsal, particularly the first few days, write everything down. There is something very disarming about teaching somebody their blocking and business and their not recording it in their scripts. More likely than not, I know I will have to give it all to them again the next time we do it. I don't mind moving slowly through the process in order to allow you to record as we go along; it is part of the process and is in no way indulgent. This way, when you go through your lines at home, you'll be reminded of when and where you move.

Another one of my biggest pet peeves is actors who criticize or make snarky comments about another actor's performance while they are backstage or in common areas. The backstage area should be a safe area and one where your fellow actors aren't judged.

If you must criticize or be snarky about another actor's performance, do it when you're away from the theater or at the bar, never in the backstage area.

I simply think it is best for morale that we support one another, and of course you wouldn't want people talking negatively about your performance while you were onstage.

David Hyslop
Production Stage Manager
CHICAGO The Musical

On another note, I recently performed in a show where one of the lead actresses was so disconnected during the performance that she was actually backstage showing other actors YouTube videos that had absolutely nothing to do with the show during the performance! How disrespectful can you be? Not only are you not concentrating on your performance, but you're distracting another actor's process! Not to mention just not being present for your fellow performers. If you are not invested in what you're doing (regardless of whether you like the piece or not), you should not have signed on to be a part of it. Trust me, there's always someone in the wings waiting for a chance.

It has also recently come to my attention that some stage managers who are new to the business might allow disrespectful behavior from actors just because they have a principal role. To this I say, please know that sometimes people will test you and you have to be a strong enough stage manager to know that folks will always try to cross the line. Once that happens, it's hard trying to bring them back. Sometimes actors just don't know the rules. Stage managers, it's up to you to be well versed as well in backstage etiquette. I know it can be hard because sometimes you have a creative team (including producers) who might not want you to rock the boat with some of their stars. But you do such a disservice to the production and the actor if you don't make sure everyone is in order. Your Actor's Equity rule book will always have your back.

The Broadway stage manager is also the equivalent of the office manager in an office job or the floor manager in a restaurant. Every office/business needs one or two people who keep everything running smoothly. Having respect for that person and knowing your responsibilities are crucial in any job. Often, your job evaluation rests on the shoulders of these people, so keeping them happy is mandatory. I'm not saying you have to kiss up to them, but know what your duties are and carry them out professionally.

Tardiness is not tolerated in any business. Energy and purpose when performing a job/task/assignment is a must. Be on point, as they say. If you become known as a slouch, there's a chance that label will follow you everywhere. Professionalism is a learned skill. You have to want to be the best you can be and shouldn't assume you know everything—especially if you don't really have the experience yet.

Keep in mind your manager (stage manager) is probably watching you when you're not aware. When you're casually criticizing a coworker or gossiping around the water cooler, you might be watched, and managers might get the idea you're just trouble.

Once again, gratitude goes a long way. A smile and a please and thank you should not be a thing of the past. It won't hurt to say it to managers as well as coworkers, because one day it might be up to those same people to give you a job somewhere down the line in your career. I can't tell you how many times I have had to audition for someone I was in the chorus with once and it was now up to them whether I got the job or not!

Here's an example of how you never know who can help you in your career. While I was writing this book in 2016, I was contacted by a company manager I had worked with on Broadway over 10 years prior at Smokey Joe's Cafe. She called to say she had heard that the original creative team from the Broadway production of After Midnight was now mounting it for Norwegian Cruise Line and she thought I would make a great Star Singer. Not two days later another friend called to say, "Your ears must have been burning. I'm now head of casting for Norwegian Cruise Line; your name came up for the Star Singer role and I told them we were friends!" Now, this is a perfect example of staying on good terms no matter who you're working with. You see, my friend who was now casting this show was in the ensemble of CHICAGO The Musical on Broadway when I played the lead role of Velma Kelly back in 2003!

Because I'm a firm believer of "Never burn bridges because you never know what the Universe has in store for you," I have now found a new home with After Midnight on Norwegian Cruise Line.

I'm also a believer that you must stay focused and always go that extra mile. If there is a role you might want to understudy, learn those lines as well. You just never know when the question might come up, "Can someone stand in for so-and-so?" You'll be able to raise your hand and say, "I know those lines."

A few more tips: If a project is due at noon, have it ready by 11:30 if possible. Don't be afraid to admit what you don't know and ask questions. That's what your manager (stage or otherwise) is there for. It's always better to take a little extra time for clarity than to think you know it all and have to go back and redo!

Musical Director

One of my main issues is how do you teach quality? How do you teach musicians and actors what quality is? I have a few young people I help with their recordings and they have no idea what a quality sound is AND they're not even interested.

Another issue is sometimes our older, more seasoned performers get so caught up in what used to be that they're not open to change, which can make rehearsal and back-stage life challenging. I'm not sure what can be done, what I should do; is this the time I should speak out and let you know what I'm feeling?

But my main three concerns are 1. Be prepared. Ask yourself, Did I do my homework for the next day's work? Am I prepared? 2. Make sure you're perceived in a positive light. Did I do everything I could for a positive outcome? 3. Don't be so quick tempered. Know that not everyone reacts to situations the same way as you. But if you take a moment before reacting, many times a situation can be defused.

Zane Mark
Tony Award–winning Musical Director/Conductor
Motown; Dirty Rotten Scoundrels;
Bring in the Noise, Bring in the Funk

I remember being so intimidated when I landed my first show and had to learn the music. I consider myself a dancer who can sing, and though I'm not a sight reader, I do have a good ear.

This means I can't just look at the sheet music for the first time and read what's on the page (I truly admire those who can), but if you play it for me I can remember my parts. Or I will record it and by the time I have my next rehearsal I'll know it.

> *As a musical director, nothing aggravates me more than having to backtrack and totally re-teach parts to someone who has clearly not done their work outside of rehearsal. It is your responsibility to come to work prepared to do what was taught in rehearsal the day before. That means you need to schedule in time between rehearsals to practice what was taught, and it is your responsibility to get what you need in order to do that. If your sight reading skills aren't so great, or you don't have access to a keyboard, you may want to ask the musical director or pianist to allow you to record your part separately so that you can practice along to it. Whether you look at it as practicing, woodshedding or just plain doing homework, this time is critical to the process and your success in the production.*
>
> *Your work day doesn't end when rehearsal is over; it ends when you finish successfully practicing the material that was covered in that day's rehearsal.*
>
> e'Marcus Harper-Short
> *Black Nativity, Invisible Life*

I realize being able to sing by ear can be a blessing; if you ever happen to drop all your music during a reading or showcase of a show where you're allowed to have your script and music with you, you still have it all in your head! I can't tell you how many times a rehearsal has had to come to a screeching halt because someone's script and/or score is all over the floor.

Also, many times for me it's a lot easier to learn lyrics once I'm up on my feet blocking the scene with the director. It allows me to put the action in a scene with a specific lyric.

Dance Captain

I've been blessed to work with amazing directors, choreographers and musical directors (the creative team). But having spent many, many years as a dancer, I always gravitated to the choreographers and associate choreographers. This is probably what led me to also be dance captain and assistant to the choreographer in many of the shows I've done.

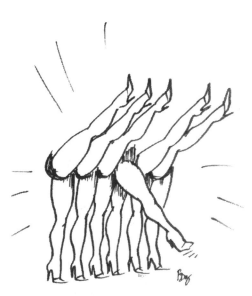

While I never wanted to be a choreographer, I was always amazed at the choreography process.

When I was coming up, you were not allowed to videotape anything in rehearsal. Everything was either remembered in your head or you had your own style of writing it down (dance notation). Things today are so much easier when you can just video everything. But I feel it sometimes takes away from the uniqueness of using your sight, brain and body. If you have to constantly look at your notes or video before you can teach choreography, you'll be at a loss if one day you don't have access to them and you have to teach the choreography or blocking. Being able to retain and recall choreography from memory is truly a lost talent.

Part of my job when I worked on Broadway in Dreamgirls was as dance captain. The dance captain is in charge of keeping the choreography clean and fresh looking. Once the show is frozen (no more changes can be made), the dance captain watches the show, making sure everything looks orderly and uniform. I still know about 80 percent of that show's choreography.

I remember one of the perks of having to watch Dreamgirls almost every night was seeing Jennifer Holliday sing "And I Am Telling You." What a performance!

My advice for performers from the perspective of dance captain is:

1. Be ready and open to change. Tech time is really for the technical crew to get their shot at the show. Something we had rehearsed before may not work now, so trust we will fix it later.

2. Trust your dance captain's eye. We get to watch the show knowing the vision the choreographer had in mind. What may feel good on you might not be the look the choreographer was going for. Respect them like you

respect the director.

One of my biggest challenges as dance captain was having to give dance notes to my peers. There's a fine line, because one minute you're laughing as friends and the next you're telling them what to do. I had a few incidents that were challenging, but for the most part my friends respected my position. So do your dance captain/friend a favor by showing respect for their position. Know where friend and business begin and end. At the end of the day, your friend also has a job to get done.

I have had the wonderful opportunity to see this business from many angles, from my first Broadway show in the chorus of Guys and Dolls to my first role as a true leading lady in Smokey Joe's Cafe. I have been out front in the audition process as well as "behind the table," as they say, having to be the one to audition friends.

But along the way I never felt I knew everything. On many levels, I'm still learning. With every new job or Broadway show, I'm learning. If you ever get to the point where you think you have "made it," think again.

Here's more wonderful feedback from someone in the trenches!

I was chosen by Ann Reinking to be dance captain for the national tour of CHICAGO in 1997 and later on Broadway, and around 2005 I was asked to be associate choreographer. Part of my job is to rehearse and give notes to the company.

Sometimes I will run up against a performer who is unable or unwilling to take the note and I have to do my best to help them process what it is that I need in order for the show to run smoothly. Once I was rehearsing Chita Rivera (the original Velma Kelly) for the role of Roxie Hart.

One day Ann stopped into rehearsal and the two of them danced "Nowadays" and "Hot Honey Rag." When they were done they looked at me and said, "Okay, please give us your notes." WHAT???? I was taken aback just a bit.

Here were these two legends of theater who had both performed in CHICAGO for another legend, the original director and creator Bob Fosse, and they were asking ME for notes.

I tell this story because it is a wonderful example of not feeling ENTITLED by bringing your ego into the rehearsal process. These two women could have noted themselves or not have asked for notes at all, but that's not who they are as people or as performers. Chita and Annie always want to do and be better at their craft. They are always look-ing to raise their game onstage and off. I have gotten more flack from much less established performers!

So my advice to young performers is, come to play and leave your ego outside the room. Please study EVERYTHING you can—theater is evolving and your skill set needs to be on point. This business is about persever-ance. We have been lulled into this false sense that success is overnight due to reality TV and other factors. BEWARE! Look at those who have come before you and have long careers in theater. They built their careers show by show, audition by audition, moment by moment. Stay eager but

prepare yourself for the long haul.
   My pet peeves:

1. *Young performers who say to me, "OMG, I saw you perform when I was in elementary school!" URGH! Haha!*

2. *Performers who STOP studying.*

3. *Performers who want the preverbal "IT" right now and have no idea of perseverance.*

4. *Performers who do not use the rehearsal process to its fullest.*

5. *Any performer who feels ENTITLED.*

6. *Performers who are not willing to take direction and feel the need to defend themselves. They need to SHUT UP and LISTEN!*

7. *Performers who are undisciplined during the audition process.*

8. *Performers who don't know the rich history of their chosen field.*

9. *Performers who do not understand that they are there to fulfill the vision of the creative team.*

10. *Performers who say, "I'll try!"*

Gregory Butler
Associate Choreographer
CHICAGO The Musical

During my stint on Broadway as Velma Kelly in CHICAGO The Musical, I had the pleasure of working with Bebe Neuwirth as my Roxie! I was so excited yet nervous to play opposite her (she'd won the Tony award for her role as Velma Kelly) and she was known for her dedication to and for the craft. My biggest concern was whether I would do it right and if she would approve of my interpretation of Velma Kelly. I quickly learned Bebe was entirely focused on her new role as Roxie and our relationship as these two characters. We jelled into what we needed to be for these roles and actually became great friends with mutual respect for each other's talents.

Here are some of Bebe's thoughts on backstage etiquette.

Please do not vocalize after Half Hour has been called. If you need to find a secluded corner to hum to yourself quietly, by all means try to find one. Otherwise, your vocalizing warm up is something to take care of at home or before Half Hour.

Check your props before the show begins. During the performance, after you've used your prop, put it back in its designated place on the prop table, or hand it off to a crew member as prearranged. Your offstage blocking is just as important as your onstage blocking.

Respect your costume. Do not eat or take breaks in your costume. Hang it up when you are finished with it, or place it in the laundry as the Costume Department requests.

Respect the crew. These people are your colleagues!

Do not be late for rehearsal or any calls. And if you've got a dance rehearsal, be warmed up and ready to dance full out—before it starts. (The same goes for a vocal call; you should be ready to sing in full voice.)

Please do not chew gum in rehearsal.

Please do not yawn in rehearsal.

It all comes down to a matter of respect. Respect for the theater. Respect for your fellow performers, respect for your crew, respect for your director, choreographer, conductor, stage managers. Respect for your audience. Respect for yourself.

Bebe Neuwirth

Tony and Emmy Award winner

Cheers, CHICAGO The Musical

One last note on stepping into a role. Very seldom will your director even want you to play the character exactly as the previous actor did. They want you to bring your take and talent into the arena. Walter Bobbie, the director of CHICAGO on Broadway, told me, "Brenda, I hired you for what you bring to the table." I'll always remember that because it gave me permission to be creative.

Dressing Room
(Home away from Home)

I can't even begin to tell you the many different dressing room situations I have had! From unisex dressing areas at the Urban Arts Corps (and mainly in non-union shows) to sharing space with two dogs!! Yes, that's what I said—DOGS!

At Dreamgirls we were known as the Ladies of Room 10. It was Brenda Pressley, Vanessa Bell Calloway, Candy Darling and me, in barely a 12' x 12' dressing room with major costumes and two small dogs. Yet we never had any problems with space (or the lack thereof) because there was a code of common respect. (A bit of Dreamgirls trivia for you: the two dogs, YoYo and Jason, belonged to me. They were walked by Phylicia Rashaad as the "Dog Act," but if you blinked you would miss them. What a time that was. Especially when they pooped on the stage! But I digress...)

I learned so many lessons in my time with the Dreamgirls production, many of which didn't fully make sense until I became older. I realized there were things taking place that were actually more than just the "etiquette" of working and living in this world. One experience that will always keep a special place in my heart and mind was with an older woman in the ensemble.

She was much older than us and we used to laugh because we thought she seemed so out of touch with what was going on.

When things went crazy backstage, she would often be the calm one with words of wisdom. Or she would just laugh at us.

Sometimes we would see her mood change at the drop of a hat or she would break out in a sweat for no reason. Of course I now know those were hot flashes. At the time we were too young to have any compassion for her and would just laugh and dismiss it. Now…well, let's just say I know firsthand what a hot flash is!

Space Taming

Keep in mind that your roommates have rights too. Sometimes we forget or have never been taught. When sharing a dressing room and dressing table, you always have to be aware of how much space you're taking up.

Your dressing table space can explode and seep out onto your neighbor's area before you know it. It would be wise to make use of trays that can store small items and keep things in order.

The rule of thumb is, in a very crowded dressing room with minimum dressing table space, try to use a hand towel as a mat and place all your things within that space. Most of all, be aware of your surroundings. If things get out of hand, address it with kindness, not attitude, because if you're lucky and it's a hit show, you might be sitting next to these people for a long time. In our case, it was almost four years. Dreamgirls had a great run!

Important: Do not use one another's makeup, makeup brushes, lipstick, eye liner, eyebrow pencils, stick deodorant, etc. It's a sure way to spread unwanted viruses and diseases. I don't care how close you are as friends; sharing this stuff is just not safe, period!

Also remember to clean your makeup brushes at least once every two weeks, depending on how much you use them. Don't use makeup sponges more than three times. When they are covered in makeup, throw them away.

Do not put your dance shoes on the table where you put on your makeup. That's just so unsanitary! This may sound obvious, but I've seen it happen.

Playing Music

The dressing room is a place of preparation. Therefore, unless everyone has agreed to certain music being played, it should be a fairly quiet zone. Now that's not to say you won't find a dressing room situation where everyone loves the same music and doesn't mind an energetic, crazy prep time. But you better believe there will be a day when someone just needs a little quiet time before their show and that could become difficult.

It wasn't until after my run in an Off-Broadway show called Little Ham that I realized how abusive we were to our dressing room neighbors with our nightly ritual of playing a song that was quite popular at the time called "Move Bitch" by Ludacris.

We would sing along at the top of our lungs without regard for the people next door. Luckily we did have the common sense to only sing it before half hour, yet it was disrespectful and I'm sure annoying to others. Again, this was before iPods, iPhones, etc.

It's your responsibility to purchase a good set of headphones if you need your music to be loud! It is not your roommate's responsibility to find earplugs to drown out your music or loud talking.

Phone Calls

In 1976, on my first Broadway show, Guys and Dolls, cell phones weren't an option. They hadn't even been created yet! So you had to make sure you had enough change for the pay phone at the stage door. At intermission it was first come first served, and there was always a line. My dressing room was all the way on the top floor, so by the time I got out of costume and back down to the phone, intermission was often over. Now, I'm sure we have all experienced those times when we were on public transportation, at a movie or standing on a line, and someone was on the phone talking at the top of their lungs or had their call on speakerphone. Just the other day I was on a crowded bus where someone was on the phone and decided to put the call on speaker because, as she stated, "I ain't got no headphones so..."

That's exactly how it can feel in a shared dressing room. Be mindful and step out of the room for your calls if they get a bit loud or energetic. But also be mindful in all common areas. You are not at home!

Vocal Warm Up

Again, all of your vocal warming up really should be done before you enter the theater. Half hour is not the time for your full warm up. A gentle bit of humming is okay, but a full-on vocal warm up is out of the question. Can you imagine a cast of over 30 performers trying to warm up at the same time during half hour? Crazy!

You must respect the fact that every actor has his or her own way to prepare for a performance. There are Equity rules regarding dressing room/prep space conduct, but here are a list of things you definitely want to remember:

1. *Some actors don't like loud music playing as they prepare for a performance; wear your earbuds.*

2. *Some actors don't care to engage in conversation before a performance; leave them alone.*

3. *No one wants to hear you vocalizing in their ear, NO ONE!*

4. *You don't have permission to bring guests into the dressing room, so don't.*

5. *You are NOT allowed to touch anything that belongs to another actor!*

e'Marcus Harper-Short
Musical Director
Black Nativity, Invisible Life

Hairspray/Perfume/Cologne

There's nothing worse than inhaling a nose and mouth full of hairspray, perfume or cologne. It can literally take your breath away and cause throat irritations. And that's the last thing you need before you perform.

Common courtesy would be to step outside the dressing room or into the hair prep room if you need to spray hairspray. When applying your favorite scent, remember a little can go a long way. Just think if everyone went overboard with their favorite scent—it would be pretty overwhelming.

There may come a time when your costume may become a little "ripe," as we call it (smelly), but just know, dousing it with cologne or perfume does not make it better. This is when you must go to your dresser for help. If you have to wear another actor's costume (which can happen in an understudy situation), make sure you ask that the costume be fully cleaned if time permits.

On most shows your dresser will already know this, but there are times, especially on regional shows, that it might get overlooked.

Pits, Privates And...

When you're in a public dressing room situation, you must be ever vigilant with keeping every part of your body the freshest it can be. I would rather someone pull me to the side to tell me than have everyone talking behind my back. Many times people are not aware when they carry an odor, whether it's from private areas or the mouth, and a gentle mention in private can go a long way.

I remember once we had to mention it to our stage manager and she was able to pull the actor aside and tell them. It's okay if done with love and respect.

Speaking of Smells...

Do not—I repeat, do not burn candles or incense in your dressing room at any time. Not only is it inconsiderate to your fellow actors who may not appreciate the smell, it is a FIRE HAZARD.

Bathroom "Doodie"

When we're sharing the dressing room, we sometimes find there is a common bathroom that's shared as well, and it can get smelly at times. I would suggest you do your part by being prepared with the great match trick. If you know it's going to be one of those times, have a book of match-es with you. Strike and immediately extinguish a match before and after "the deed." It will help clear the air.

Again, these rules can be easily translated for other work situations. Unless you have your own office with four walls and a door you can close, here's the deal.

Just like sharing a dressing room, when sharing office space there are several dos and don'ts everyone should follow to keep the peace:

- No borrowing items (pens, pencils, paper, paper clips, etc.) without permission.
- No loud music. Sometimes even with headphones, music can seep out. So invest in a good set.
- Keep the use of perfumes, colognes and scented lotions to a minimum.
- Personal hygiene is a must! Body and mouth odor is just wrong. Keep hands and feet (if you're allowed to wear open-toe shoes) neat and well groomed. There's nothing worse than cracked nails/polish and crusty feet.
- No gum chewing or popping.
- Keep your voice down on all phone calls.

Dressers/Wardrobe

Your dresser is not:

Your maid

Your personal assistant

Your secretary

Your housekeeper

Your servant

Yo mama!

Your dresser is there to help with your costumes and sometimes hair, so make sure you have all costume pieces and they fit properly. Dressers are your lifeline to the wardrobe supervisor, who is the lifeline to the costume designer. Any costume issues should be relayed in a calm manner.

Your costume should also be treated with respect. There should be no eating in your costume! Many times there are no replacements for costumes, so if you accidentally drop food on them it would cause a big problem. It's helpful to have a bathrobe to put on if you must eat in costume. Usually the only time you're allowed to eat or drink in a costume is if it would take too long to

undress then dress again during intermission.

When you remove your costumes, they should be left neatly on the back of your dressing chair. If you have time to hang them up yourself, that can be helpful as well, since your dresser may manage several performers.

You should absolutely not leave your costume in a pile on the floor or throw it around! Usually there are laundry baskets or mesh bags (ditty bags) for underwear. Do not just leave sweaty undergarments on the floor or hand them to your dresser!

I remember being appalled at a fellow performer when I was a member of Cats on Broadway. After dancing the "Jellicle Ball" she stepped out of her costume (a sweaty unitard) and walked away, leaving a wet heap of spandex for her dresser to pick up. Gross!

Treat your costume as if you purchased it yourself. Hang up your costume after wearing it, do not toss costume pieces on the floor, and do not purposely rip or tear costumes with the mindset that someone will simply fix it.

However, do not be afraid to tell the wardrobe crew if there is a stain or rip in the costume piece. Wardrobe is there to help performers and would prefer the honesty if a repair is needed, rather than having a piece get into worse shape over the duration of the production. Also, treating the wardrobe crew with respect is just as important as properly using costume pieces.

The more appreciative and understanding one is towards wardrobe, or any stagehand, the more a member of wardrobe will make sure a costume piece is repaired and ready for the next performance.

Sarah Greenstone
Dresser
Maltz Jupiter Theatre

I have found in many of the shows I've done that the costume designer will also try to take into consideration the performers' body type, best colors, materials they're allergic to and so on. Many times they will listen to a few suggestions, but it can be a very sensitive subject.

It's best to try to wait to be asked your opinion, then gently respond. Once the show has been frozen, it's hard to then ask for changes. And by no means should you take it upon yourself to adjust, embellish, remove/add pieces or otherwise change your costume. The costume designer has worked hard on designing the show and would like to see their work onstage as close to the way they've designed it as possible.

One of my pet peeves of working with up-and-coming actors is when the show has opened and they take it upon themselves to begin to alter the design of the show, whether that is with the costume, makeup and/or wigs. The show has been designed, implemented and approved by the director. I believe it is very disrespectful to the designer to alter their design without their consent. If there is something that an actor does not agree with it needs to be addressed prior to opening, not after the fact. What I feel most actors fail to realize is that as dressers it is our responsibility to make sure that the designer's design is not lost throughout the run of the show. That being said, trust the dressers and realize that they want you to look your best because that too reflects upon the way they are doing their job.

A recommendation that I would give to incoming actors is to enter the tech process understanding that as dressers we typically do not come in until the end of the rehearsal process. Dressers are not in fittings; therefore, the actor has more knowledge about their costume order than their dressers in many cases. Tech is a learning process for us and we are all trying to become familiar with all of the new aspects being incorporated into the show. Although during that time we may all be sleep deprived, frustrated and confused, ultimately we are all working towards the same goal: opening a great show.

Jackie Sayles
Dresser
Maltz Jupiter Theatre

It's also customary to tip your dresser at the end of the eight-show week to say thank you. The amount should be whatever is comfortable for you. Many times it will also depend on the extra little things your dresser might voluntarily do such as bringing you tea, water, lozenges, etc. I have had amazing dressers in my time. They are very special people!

In a normal workplace situation I know many people say, "I should be able to wear whatever I want to work as long as I get my work done." In some instances I agree, but for the most part

I never understand why anyone would want to come to work looking like they just rolled out of bed or are heading to or just coming from the club! Dude, don't wear that shirt three days in a row without washing it!

Hair Department

Usually you will have signed a rider with your contract stating you have to keep your hair, beard, weight and skin tone (no overtanning) the same as when you were hired. But if you will be using wigs or the production alters your hair length or color, they will be responsible for the upkeep while you are employed in the production. Should you be required to wear a wig, do not make any changes to the style of your wig. If there is a problem, make sure you see the wig master or whomever is in charge of wig maintenance. In some productions you are not allowed to put on or take off your own wig without the assistance of the wig person. Other productions might be a little less strict. Make sure you inquire ahead of time. If you have a suggestion for a wig style, make sure you share the suggestion in a respectful manner. Ultimately, it is the wig master's decision. As with your costume, never just throw a wig on the counter, chair or floor, and don't take it upon yourself to spray it with hairspray unless cleared by the wig master.

In many shows, because of the large number of wigs that are used, we often have to have set appointment times for cast members. One of my pet peeves is when performers are consistently late for their hair appointments. I find this to be very inconsiderate not only to me, the hairdresser, but to fellow performers as well. When a performer is late, it makes me late, which, in turn, causes other performers to be late. It's a snowball effect. Unprofessional.

And this is a big one! It never ceases to amaze me why performers think it's cute and fun to try on another performer's wigs. Firstly, wigs are not toys—they are very expensive and delicate. Secondly, I find it rather disgusting. Do you try on another performer's sweaty costumes? I think not. So why is it cute and fun to try on another performer's wig? Eeewwww! Again, unprofessional!

My Advice: You're the new kid on the block so sit back and watch and LEARN! Don't enter a situation thinking that you know everything about the business just because you got your first Broadway show right out of college.

Remember, many of your coworkers have been in the business for years and know a lot more than you do. They can teach you so much. So leave the "I'm hot shit" attitude back on the college campus!

Scott Mortimer
Wig Master
CHICAGO The Musical

Stagehands/Deck Crew

Your stagehands and deck crew can sometimes have your life in their hands. But it's also your responsibility to know what's going on around you backstage, onstage and in the wings. There can be times when knowing what's happening will prevent serious accidents.

Many times the stage crew will have several moving stage pieces, props and cues they are responsible for. Your cooperation and awareness can help things move along in a safe and orderly way. Make sure you know where your props are and they're returned to the same spot unless otherwise directed.

YOUR PROPS ARE NOT TOYS!

So don't play with them, take them to your dressing room or leave them around haphazardly.

If there is a problem with a prop, let your assistant stage manager know ASAP. If it's an emergency (happening the moment you're walking on/off stage), it can often be mentioned directly to the stagehand.

But rule of thumb is to mention issues to stage management. Be respectful of each crew department and its hierarchy.

I have worked with amazing crew and stagehands. While writing this book I was working on The Wiz at the Maltz Jupiter Theatre, where I actually had to fly! This can be very tricky and you must have everyone on the same page at all times! There is no playing when it comes to a performer having to be flown  several feet in the air. Flying a performer has more components than you think. In preparation for my flying as Glinda the Good Witch in The Wiz, I had to actually be measured for a harness built specifically for my body.

Once the harness was built, then the process really started, including several flying rehearsals, a safety talk and deciding what to do in case of an emergency.

As a crewman of 15 years, having worked in many types of productions, with many different people, my list would be fairly long and specific. But to paint the broad strokes and cover the typically universal scenarios, a fair amount of my pet peeves can be covered through common sense and common courtesy. As I think about them, I realize my comments would be the same to actors, crew or anyone really.

GENERAL PHILOSOPHY

- *Nobody likes a self-important, arrogant diva. Nobody.*
- *Don't build a clique barrier between cast and crew, especially when most of the crew personnel are there to keep you safe as well as make you look good. (If you're crew, understand the cast doesn't know your name or what you do, and it's probably because you've forgotten to introduce yourself or even speak to them.)*

Save the drama for the scene onstage. Everyone has problems; don't bring personal ones into the professional environment.

Before you get angry or snippy with anyone, take a moment and put yourself in their place. A 10 out of 12 for actors is usually a 16 out of 16 for the crew. We're all overworked, underpaid, sleep deprived and (the good ones) filling out dead spots in other departments simply to make the theater machine run.

When you find a person like this, VALUE THEM, because the high fives or words of appreciation you offer them may be the only compensation they get for breaking their bodies for the production.

PRACTICAL MATTERS

- *Be aware of your surroundings. Theater magic happens from every angle. There are traps in the floor, moving walls and wagons, flying pieces over your head, and crew running everywhere to make it all happen. A good crew is trying their best to look out for you, but help us help you.*

Don't bring your coffee, tea or other open container onstage. Ever. Someone has already cleaned the entire stage (probably twice) that day and really doesn't want to clean your spill or condensation ring off a set piece, prop table, or, heaven help you, an electrical box.

- *Keep your voice down backstage. You CAN be heard onstage and it's quite rude and distracting to your fellow actors onstage who are trying to work. You may also be distracting a stagehand who has a scene shift or quick change and is listening intently for their dialogue cue.*

- *During tech, know your lines and blocking and PAY ATTENTION. If everyone is on the ball, focused and looking ahead, tech runs a lot smoother, and we can all make the best of a long crappy day.*

- *Be tidy and considerate. If you miss the garbage can with your tissue, go...pick...it...up. Same goes for your green room and dressing room snacks, cigarette butts and most definitely your chewing gum. Somebody will have to clean up after you if you leave a mess, and they're probably muttering a voodoo curse on you the whole time.*

- *Be on time. Whether it's places, a wig call, mic check, makeup or what have you, someone is waiting on you and we'd ALL like to have our break or get done and home as soon as possible.*

- *Avoid brushing against soft goods and flown pieces. The rail man has enough to worry about. Touching a flown piece moves it from its linear path and creates a much larger chance for pieces to collide in the air...over YOUR head.*

- *Please don't manhandle and abuse props and set pieces. Somebody has to fix those.*
- *If crew asks or tells you to move, it's probably to keep you from getting run over by a wagon or to keep you from getting a concussion from a flown piece that's coming in.*

Ogre
Deck Crew
The Wiz
Maltz Jupiter Theatre

I must admit this is a very important section because it can literally be a life-and-death situation, or a situation that can end your career if there's an accident. I have a very good friend whose career was cut short because he accidentally fell through a trap door onstage. SO PLEASE PAY ATTENTION!

I also remember when I was doing Dreamgirls on Broadway and I was standing in the wings waiting to make an entrance, wondering where all our large set pieces had disappeared to. When I asked a stagehand, he pointed up. Sure enough, all of the set that wasn't being used at the time was hanging over our heads—thus the meaning of the words "Heads up!"

Company Manager

MONEY! MONEY! MONEY! MONEEEEY! MONEY!

Need I say more! Your company manager is in charge of your "black money" (your paycheck). I'm not sure where that

phrase came from, but on Thursday nights on Broadway (payday!) you can often hear the cries, "Thank you for my black money!"

More than likely, after the audition process you dealt with the company manager for your contract (unless you're a principal, in which case your agent worked with them).

Your company manager can help you on so many levels, from house seat orders (when you request to purchase tickets to the show that can be the best seats in the house) to helping you find a bank to cash your check if you're on the road in a small town. This is also the person that will sometimes drive you to the hospital if you get sick when out of town on tour.

I will never forget the care that both my stage manager and company manager gave me when we were on the road with CHICAGO The Musical.

We were in Canada and I had the worst stomach pain I had ever experienced. Hilary Hamilton (company manager) and her sister Marjorie (stage manager) sprang into action! They took me to emergency and waited hours with me as a battery of tests were run. They were a godsend and I will always be grateful to them.

> *I think the most important thing an actor can be is kind. Part of my job is to make any actor feel comfortable while they are in residence at the theater, and I will bend over backwards to make sure that they are having a great experience. It can be challenging to try to help someone who is unpleasant and ungrateful. I'll still take care of them, but they may not be invited back.*
>
> Rachel Blavatnik
> Company Manager
> Maltz Jupiter Theatre

Curtain Calls

I take curtain calls very seriously. I'll never forget when Michael Bennett "choreographed " the Dreamgirls curtain call. We had a very large cast, but the way he took the time to make sure it was elegant and precisioned was simply brilliant!

First of all, the bows are a part of your show. You can't spend two hours performing and then slough off the curtain call. The audience deserves your best performance all the way to the end! Unless it has been choreographed into the curtain call (bows), there is no reason for you to be talking and laughing while your fellow performers are bowing. There's no reason to be doing full-on choreography, or getting ready to make a quick getaway to catch that 10:30 train. Yes, there can be certain instances when an actor actually does have to make a train, but your audience should never know! The magic of the show should continue until the curtain comes down, the lights go out or that last actor has exited the stage. PERIOD!

In a Nutshell

There are many people willing to give "advice" who have not been in a show or experienced the culture of backstage life. My advice for new performers is to watch what goes on around you. Soak up as much positive information as possible from artists who have a great reputation and have actually been working in the business. The world behind the scenes—whether on Broadway, off Broadway, or in television—has rules and regulations that should be followed. Some rules can save lives and some are just common courtesy.

Everyone involved wants a comfortable work environment where each person and department is respected. Life backstage is a living, moving entity.

The more you know, the better your experience and the experience of the cast and crew around you. No matter how old you are, how many shows you've done or how talented you think you are, backstage etiquette is important. You should never feel you know it all or there is no more to learn. After 40 years in the business, I'm still open to learning something new. Some of the thoughts, ideas and experiences shared in this book might also keep you from being terminated and instead help you have a long, enjoyable career!

While writing this book I had the pleasure of interviewing one of my all time favorite living legends, Ms. Chita Rivera. I spent an amazing day at the feet of a master whose career has survived, thrived and is STILL flourishing. She had so many wonderful tid bits to pour into my heart and spirit. My final question to her was what would your words to these up and coming performers be?

"There's so much to tell but most of all they have to be very grateful for where they are. They must be extremely respectful and open to their fellow performers because they can't do it by themselves. Treat each other with great respect. That's the way they'll learn and have a better experience. Do their fullest. Be yourself and be as full as you are directed to be. You don't know all the answers and you are learning all the time. Every time they go into that theater they are learning and they have to be open. If they stay open they can handle things better. If you keep yourself open you'll get all kinds of goodies to do your show. You are wasting time by NOT having those ingredients."

Chita's Final words…

"Be Patient. Do what you love. Do what you can do best. Believe in those moments. Don't take yourself too serious. Keep your sense of humor because when you get slapped it's not so bad if you have a sense of humor."

Chita Rivera
Tony Award-winning Actress

I've known many people who were hired not necessarily because of their talent, but because they were easy to work with. This business is magical, with wonderful talented people, and we are all here with the same hope, and that is to have a show with a long, successful run.

My last word of advice is to also Google some of the people who have lent their opinions, quotes and experiences here. You might be surprised at the amazing body of work of these artists!

Etiquette at a Glance

Be civil to your doorman.

Stay off your phone during a table read.

Use a real paper script and pencil for recording notes and blocking.

Be mentally present at a put-in or understudy rehearsal.

Your dresser is not your maid, personal assistant, secretary, housekeeper, servant or yo mama!

Do not redesign your costume.

Do not leave your costume on the floor.

Get headphones if you need to listen to music.

Be aware of body and mouth odor.

Be on time.

Don't sign in for half hour then leave the theater.

Treat your costume as if it were your personal clothing.

Let your dresser know right away if your costume needs repairs.

Do not alter hair color, weight or skin color (overtanning).

Be respectful of every department.

Do not treat props like toys.

Don't act like a diva.

Don't build a barrier between you and the crew.

Don't bring liquids onstage—ever.

Keep your voice down in the wings.

If a crew person asks you to move, do so with no argument.

Be ready and open for change.

Trust your dance captain's eye.

Do not do your full-on vocal warm up after half hour.

Don't use too much hairspray, cologne or perfume.

Be known as a person that comes to work and does their eight shows a week.

Actors don't give other actors notes.

Do not try on other actors' wigs or headpieces.

Do not use other actors' makeup, lipstick, eyeliner, etc.

Your curtain call is part of your show.

Glossary of Theater Terms

APRON

The area in front of the stage.

ASSISTANT STAGE MANAGER (ASM)

The person working directly under the Production Stage Manager (PSM) who usually has the same skills and would step in if the PSM was not available.

BIOGRAPHY (Bio)

A paragraph in Playbill explaining each actor's theater credits. Usually each actor in the production gets to supply a short bio and a head shot.

BLOCKING

Places, positions and walking patterns given to performers onstage.

BODY MIC

A small microphone attached to the costume or under a wig, used to amplify the actor's voice.

CAT WALK

A narrow, often elevated, walkway, as on the sides of a bridge or in the flies above a theater stage.

CENTER STAGE

The location in the middle of the stage halfway between stage left and stage right.

CHEATING

The practice of turning one's body towards the audience even while keeping the head facing one's scene partner. Cheating is usually necessary for the audience to really see the actors and view the scene.

CLEAR THE STAGE

A direction given to all actors, musicians and technicians to leave the stage area prior to the beginning of a play.

COMPANY MANAGER

The person in charge of negotiating contracts and dispersing weekly/monthly paychecks.

CONDUCTOR

The person in charge of leading/conducting the orchestra and performers during the show.

COSTUME DESIGNER

The person in charge of the design of the costumes for the production.

COVER

Another term for understudy.

CREATIVE TEAM

The director, choreographer, musical director and costume designer.

CROSSOVER

The area just behind the stage used to cross from one side of the stage to the other. Some crossovers are under the stage.

CUE-TO-CUE

When the lighting or sound crew runs through each of its cues to check for errors. This is done without actors onstage.

CURTAIN CALL

When the actors come to the front of the stage to bow at the end of a performance.

DANCE CAPTAIN

Person in charge of keeping the show's choreography clean.

DANCE NOTATION

A way for dancers, choreographers and dance captains to write down and keep track of dance steps.

DECK

Stage area.

DIRECTOR

The person who directs a show. In most cases, the director has the final say on all aspects of the production.

DITTY BAG

A mesh laundry bag given to each actor where undergarments are placed to be laundered after each show.

DOOR MAN/WOMAN

The person who sits at the stage door to receive packages and announce guests of the performers.

DOWNSTAGE

The location near the front of the stage towards the audience.

DRAMATURGE

A theatrical scholar. During production, a dramaturge is responsible for historical accuracy and for conforming to the vision of the absent, or deceased, playwright.

DRESS REHEARSAL

A rehearsal of the show from top to bottom in costume, with music and sound. Usually without an audience, but often friends and family are invited to the final dress rehearsal.

DRY TECH

When the running crew practices each scene change without actors on-stage. This is done to ensure each scene change can be completed swiftly and quietly.

EXIT

Stage direction which specifies which person goes offstage.

FIGHT CALL

Usually a few minutes during half hour when all staged fighting is rehearsed for safety. This time is also now used for any dance lifts that are given a little extra time.

FOOT OF THE STAGE
The edge of the stage towards the audience. There are usually numbers placed here so the actors can judge their spacing and blocking during their performance.

FOURTH WALL
An imaginary surface at the edge of the stage through which the audience watches a performance. If a character speaks directly to the audience or walks on/off the stage, this is known as "breaking the fourth wall."

FREEZING THE SHOW
The time after all rehearsals are finished when no more changes are made to the show.

FULL HOUSE
The state of all of the seats being filled; the state of the entire audience section being filled to capacity.

GLOW TAPE
A glow-in-the-dark tape used on the floor of the stage that marks the positions where actors should stand.

HALF HOUR
The 30 minutes before the performance begins when all performers must sign in and prepare for the show.

HEAD SHOT
A photo of an actor, usually shot from the shoulders up.

HEADS UP!
A term of warning used to call attention to overhead danger.

HOUSE LEFT
The area of the audience that would be on your right-hand side if you are onstage facing the audience.

HOUSE RIGHT

The area of the audience that would be on your left-hand side if you are onstage facing the audience.

HOUSE SEATS

Seats in the audience of the theater held specifically for the company of the production to purchase. These are usually the best seats.

IMPROVISATION

When an actor who is "in character" makes up action or dialog without prior scripting.

INTERMISSION

A break between acts (usually between the first and second acts, but some plays have three or more acts).

INVESTOR

A person who puts up the financing for the production to be done.

JUMPER CABLE

An extension cable with a stagepin head.

LEADING LADY

The actress playing the largest role in the cast performed by a female (or originally intended for that purpose).

LEADING MAN

The actor playing the largest role in the cast performed by a male (or originally intended for that purpose).

LEGS

Masking curtains hung vertically and parallel to the sides of the proscenium. Legs define the sides of the performing area and hide offstage areas from the view of the audience.

LIGHTING DESIGNER

The person who designs the lighting (colors, intensity, mood) for the production.

MASKING

Drapery or flats used to frame the stage and prevent the audience from seeing the backstage areas.

MEET AND GREET
A meeting of the entire production company (actors, singers and creative team), usually on the first day of rehearsal.

MUSICAL DIRECTOR
The director of the orchestra of a musical.

OFFSTAGE
The area just before you enter the playing area of the stage.

ORCHESTRA PIT
The area usually located on a lower level directly in the front of the stage. It can often extend under the stage.

PACKED HOUSE
Full house.

PLACES
The direction for all actors, musicians and technicians to go to their proper position and be ready for the beginning of a play or scene.

PLAYBILL
A publication handed out to audience members as they enter the theater that provides information on the production and the cast.

PRODUCER
Someone who finds financing for and supervises the making and presentation of a show (play or film or program or similar work).

PRODUCTION ASSISTANT
The person who assists the Production Stage Manager with the general running of rehearsals.

PRODUCTION STAGE MANAGER (PSM)
The person in charge of all aspects of running the production. Usually one of the first people hired by the creative team.

PROP MASTER
The person in charge of gathering and setting whatever items will be

used in the production.

PROPS

Items (such as furniture) used for scenes in the production.

PUT-IN REHEARSAL

A rehearsal held for a new actor joining the show.

QUICK CHANGE

The short time between scenes when a performer has to make a costume change.

RAKED STAGE

When the set inclines as it goes upstage. Often used in the past (especially in Shakespeare's time) to force the perspective of the stage picture.

READ THROUGH

A reading of the entire play or act without blocking.

RE-BLOCK

When a performer's scene, entrance or exit has to be adjusted (or restaged) from its original staging.

RUNNING CREW

Backstage members (not actors) who help run the technical aspects of the show, such as the prop master, electrician, spot operator and stage managers.

RUN THROUGH

A rehearsal of the show from beginning to end.

SET DESIGNER

The person who designs how the set and props should look.

SOLD OUT

When the number of tickets sold for a performance is equal to or greater than the number of available seats.

SOUND CHECK

The time before the show begins when all microphone sound levels are checked.

SOUND DESIGNER

The person who decides how the production should sound to the audience and actors.

SOUND ENGINEER

The person in charge of supplying the equipment needed to make the sound the way the sound designer imagined. Also in charge of any special sound effects such as sirens, thunder, rainfall, etc.

SPIKE MARK

Pieces of colored tape place on the floor of the stage to mark where actors stand and props/set pieces are placed.

SPOTLIGHT (Follow Spot)

A single light usually from the back of the audience that shines on and follows one specific actor onstage.

STAGE LEFT

The location to the left of center stage if you're onstage facing the audience.

STAGE RIGHT

The location to the right of center stage if you're onstage facing the audience.

STANDBY

A male or female actor that performs if the contracted actor is unable to perform due to illness or time off from the production. This person does not have to be at the theater every night. They would call to make sure the actor they're covering is signed in and ready to perform.

STANDING OVATION

When the audience stands and claps at the end of a performance. A higher form of praise than normal applause.

STANDING ROOM

A space where people can stand to watch a performance, especially if all the seats are filled.

STANDING ROOM ONLY (SRO)

When every seat in the audience has been sold and occupied, tickets are sold to audience members who will stand to watch the performance.

STRIKE

To remove a set piece or prop from the stage ("Strike that chair"). To "strike the show" is to disassemble the entirety of the set, return all equipment to storage and leave the venue as it was before the show was set up. May be used as a noun to refer to the event at which the show is struck.

SUPPORTING CAST

Actors who are not playing major parts.

SWING DANCER

A male or female dancer who learns all the choreography and steps in when another dancer is ill or out of the show.

TABLE READ

When the entire cast and creative team sit around a table and read through the script. Usually done the first day of rehearsal.

TAP MIC

Microphones attached to a dancer's tap shoes to amplify their tapping sound while dancing.

TECH

Technical rehearsal.

TEN OUT OF TWELVE (10 out of 12)

The number of hours performers can rehearse (10) out of a 12-hour work day.

UNDERSTUDY

A male or female actor that performs if the contracted actor is unable to perform due to illness or time off from the production. This actor also usually has a part in the production that is performed nightly.

UPSTAGE

The location to the back of the stage.

VELCRO
The brand name of a type of fastening tape consisting of opposing pieces of fabric—one piece with a dense arrangement of tiny nylon hooks and the other with a dense nylon pile—that interlock when pressed together. Used as a closure on garments, luggage, etc., in place of buttons, zippers and the like. Especially used in theater for costume quick changes.

VOCAL ARRANGER
The person who arranges what notes the singers will sing.

WARDROBE SUPERVISOR
The person in charge of keeping all the costumes looking their best for the production.

WIG DESIGNER
The person who designs how the wigs and hair should look for the production.

WIG MASTER
The person in charge of keeping all the wigs and headpieces looking their best for the production.

WINDOW
The open space between two actors standing side by side.

WING 1
The area located directly offstage closest to the stage.

WING 2
The area located offstage directly upstage from wing 1.

WING 3
The area located offstage directly upstage of wing 2.

ZERO
A place on stage that's halfway between stage left and stage right. Where every actor dreams of being—center stage.

About the Author

Brenda Braxton—author, singer, dancer, actress—has had a theater career that has taken her from chorus girl to leading lady. She is a native New Yorker and graduate of the High School for the Performing Arts. In 1976 she auditioned for and joined her first Broadway show, GUYS AND DOLLS. She was featured on Broadway in SMOKEY JOE'S CAFE, where she was nominated for a Tony Award and the recipient of the NAACP Theater Award, Chicago's Jefferson Award and Grammy for Best Cast Album. In 2003 she joined the Broadway cast of CHICAGO THE MUSICAL in the starring role of Velma Kelly playing opposite Usher, Bebe Neuwirth, Rita Wilson and Brian McKnight. A few of her other Broadway credits include JELLY'S LAST JAM, CATS, LEGS DIAMOND and the original production of DREAMGIRLS.

In realizing the importance of giving back, she founded a not-for-profit organization called Leading Ladies Just for Teens (LLJFT), which holds seminars geared toward empowering young girls to be the best they can be. Leading Ladies began in 1996 at the Virginia Theater, while Brenda was there starring in SMOKEY JOE'S CAFE, with a series of seminars designed to encourage, challenge and inspire young girls to dream and set goals.

For her work as founder of LLJFT she received the Dr. Martin Luther King "Living the Dream" award given by New York's Governor Pataki, the Josephine Baker Award from the National Council of Negro Women and the Community Service Award given by the National Association of Negro Business Women.

In 2015 Ms. Braxton launched ACT 2… NOW WHAT? seminars for women over 50 looking to start over and become the leading lady of their own lives. Writing this book has been part of Brenda's Act 2, along with performing in AFTER MIDNIGHT aboard Norwegian Cruise Line's Escape.

Brenda believes it's so important to hand down the traditions and positive work ethics of successful performers who've come before us. She says, "It's not just about the work, it's about longevity!"

43602870R00058

Made in the USA
Middletown, DE
13 May 2017